BRIDAL SHOWER

MEMORIES

BY SANDRA BARK

WARNER BOOKS

An AOL Time Warner Company

CONTENTS

H o w   t o   U s e   T h i s   B o o k

◉ This journal was designed to be used at the bridal shower and for the bride to use as a personal diary before her wedding.

◉ Hosts can choose to fill in the couple's history before the shower (the groom can be useful for this!) or ask the bride questions at the shower.

◉ The guest section of the journal can be filled in during the shower. Guests should sign in and write their full addresses when they arrive, and the journal can be passed around during activities. Hosts can let guests know in advance that they'll be sharing a memory, some advice, and some personal words with the bride, or guests can be surprised when they arrive.

◉ As gifts are unwrapped, one of the hosts or guests should keep track of the presents in the gifts section.

◉ The journal section at the end is just for the bride—and so are the check boxes in the gifts section. Use them to make sure you send thank-you notes to everyone!

"Where there is great love there are always miracles."

—WILLA CATHER

THE HISTORY

OF THE

BRIDAL SHOWER

ONCE UPON A TIME a young Dutch girl fell in love with a man who had a kind heart and a handsome face, but little in the way of worldly possessions. All who knew him adored him, for he was so good and gentle that whenever he came upon someone in need, he would always share his meager portion with them.

She loved him for his sweet nature and his great beauty, and did not care that he was only a miller, while she was the daughter of a wealthy and powerful man.

But her father, a wealthy townsman, had already selected a groom for her. When the miller approached him to ask for his daughter's hand in marriage, he flew into a rage and barred the miller from ever laying eyes on his daughter again. The girl was full of grief, for she truly loved the miller, and loved her father also. She pleaded with him. She tried to reason with him. But her father was known throughout the village as an obstinate man, and he refused to see why she would choose a man other than the respectable, well-to-do landowner he had picked out for her.

At night he could hear her crying, but he hardened his resolve and said to himself, "The love that she speaks of will wither with age, but the man I have chosen for her owns land as far as the eye can see, and flocks of sheep with wool as white as the hair on my own head."

He told his daughter that if she did not listen to him, if she did not marry the groom he had selected, she would be his daughter no longer, and would forfeit any claim to his fortune, including her dowry. "If you go to nothing," he told her, "you go with nothing."

But his daughter was wiser than he about the ways of the heart and knew she would marry the miller who never hesitated to share his bread with the poor. Still, she could not stop crying, not for the loss of her fortune but for the rift that had settled within her small family.

When the townspeople, who revered the miller for his generous spirit, heard of the girl's tears, they gathered to see what they could do. The miller, who had always given to them, needed their help. While they did not have much, they all had something they could contribute to help the young couple start their life together.

They came to the mill in a long procession, all of them bearing gifts and good wishes. The miller could scarcely believe it, but the girl nodded her head sagely. "He who gives everything will never be without," she whispered, and they thanked the townspeople profusely as a pile of coverlets, porcelain, and cooking utensils grew at their feet.

When the procession of people had tapered, the two were amazed at the bounty their neighbors had shared with them. A party sprung up, and when her father heard the sounds of rejoicing, he came to the mill. When he saw all that the townspeople had done, he felt great shame. With heavy legs, with outstretched arms, he approached them. His daughter ran to him, and they embraced with great tenderness.

To make up for his coldness, he decided to give the young couple a fine house to live in. To thank the town for showering his daughter and soon to be son-in-law with gifts, he made a magnificent feast in celebration of the marriage, and invited all of the town's inhabitants, young and old and rich and poor alike.

And the bride and groom lived happily ever after.

"Life is partly what we make of it, and partly what it is made by the friends whom we choose."

—TEHYI HSIEH

NICOLE ELIZABETH HOFF

_____ ' S

S H O W E R

H O S T S :

D A T E   O F   S H O W E R :

_____

L O C A T I O N :

_____

_____

_____

_____

_____

_____

MENU

(If the shower is a potluck, why not write down who brought which dish?)

_____

_____

_____

_____

_____

_____

_____

_____

_____

_____

WEDDING CEREMONY

Date:

_____

Location:

_____

_____

_____

_____

WEDDING RECEPTION

Date:

_____

Location:

_____

_____

_____

_____

"I've loved you since the first moment I saw you. I guess maybe I even loved you before I saw you."

—MONTGOMERY CLIFT,
in *A Place in the Sun*

WHEN _end Feb._ MET _March of 2005_

FIRST MEETING

_____

_____

_____

_____

_____

_____

_____

_____

_____

_____

_____

_____

FIRST DATE

_____

_____

_____

_____

_____

_____

_____

_____

_____

_____

_____

_____

FIRST KISS

_____

_____

_____

_____

_____

_____

_____

_____

_____

_____

_____

THE PROPOSAL!

"Close friends contribute to our personal growth. They also contribute to our personal pleasure, making the music sound sweeter, the wine taste richer, the laughter ring louder because they are there."

— JUDITH VIORST

GUESTS

Names and addresses of our guests

N A M E :

A D D R E S S :

N A M E :

A D D R E S S :

N A M E :

A D D R E S S :

N A M E :

A D D R E S S :

N A M E : _____

A D D R E S S : _____

_____

_____

N A M E : _____

A D D R E S S : _____

_____

_____

N A M E : _____

A D D R E S S : _____

_____

_____

NAME: _____

ADDRESS: _____

_____

_____

NAME: _____

ADDRESS: _____

_____

_____

NAME: _____

ADDRESS: _____

_____

_____

"Call it a clan, call it a network, call it a tribe, call it a family.
Whatever you call it, whoever you are, you need one."

—JANE HOWARD

N A M E : _____

A D D R E S S : _____

_____

_____

N A M E : _____

A D D R E S S : _____

_____

_____

N A M E : _____

A D D R E S S : _____

_____

_____

N A M E : _____

A D D R E S S : _____

_____

_____

N A M E :

A D D R E S S :

N A M E :

A D D R E S S :

N A M E :

A D D R E S S :

NAME:

ADDRESS:

NAME:

ADDRESS:

NAME:

ADDRESS:

NAME:

ADDRESS:

NAME:

ADDRESS:

_____

_____

NAME:

ADDRESS:

_____

_____

NAME:

ADDRESS:

_____

_____

NAME:

ADDRESS:

_____

_____

"Friendship is a serious affection; the most sublime of all affections, because it is founded on principle, and cemented by time."

—MARY WOLLSTONECRAFT

NAME:

ADDRESS:

NAME:

ADDRESS:

NAME:

ADDRESS:

N A M E :

A D D R E S S :

N A M E :

A D D R E S S :

N A M E :

A D D R E S S :

NAME:

ADDRESS:

NAME:

ADDRESS:

NAME:

ADDRESS:

NAME:

ADDRESS:

"Although all wedding presents belong to the bride, she generally words her letters of thanks as though they belonged equally to the groom, especially if they have been sent by particular friends of his."

—EMILY POST

GIFTS

Gift: From:

☐ _____   _____

☐ _____   _____

☐ _____   _____

☐ _____   _____

☐ _____   _____

☐ _____   _____

☐ _____   _____

"Remember, the greatest gift is not found in a store nor under a tree, but in the hearts of true friends."

—CINDY LEW

Gift: From:

☐ _____   _____

☐ _____   _____

☐ _____   _____

☐ _____   _____

☐ _____   _____

$\mathcal{G}$ift: $\mathcal{F}$rom:

☐ _____   _____

☐ _____   _____

☐ _____   _____

☐ _____   _____

☐ _____   _____

Gift:

From:

- [ ] _____ _____
- [ ] _____ _____
- [ ] _____ _____
- [ ] _____ _____
- [ ] _____ _____
- [ ] _____ _____
- [ ] _____ _____

"Giving presents is a talent; to know what a person wants, to know when and how to get it, to give it lovingly and well."

—PAMELA GLENCONNER

Gift: ## From:

☐ _____   _____

☐ _____   _____

☐ _____   _____

☐ _____   _____

☐ _____   _____

☐ _____   _____

Gift: _From:_

☐ _____   _____

☐ _____   _____

☐ _____   _____

☐ _____   _____

☐ _____   _____

☐ _____   _____

☐ _____   _____

☐ _____   _____

☐ _____   _____

"The richness of life lies in memories
we have forgotten."

—CESARE PAVESE

MEMORIES

"It's a pleasure to share one's memories. Everything remembered is dear, endearing, touching, precious."

—SUSAN SONTAG

"In memory, everything seems to happen to music."

—TENNESSEE WILLIAMS

"To love and be loved is to feel the sun from both sides."

—DAVID VISCOTT

PERSONAL

NOTES

"Without friends no one would choose to live, though he had all other goods."

—ARISTOTLE

"There was a definite process by which one made people into friends, and it involved talking to them and listening to them for hours at a time."

—Rebecca West

"No distance of place or lapse of time can lessen the friendship of those who are thoroughly persuaded of each other's worth."

—ROBERT SOUTHEY

"A successful marriage requires falling in love many times, always with the same person."

—Mignon McLaughlin

ADVICE

_____

_____

_____

_____

_____

_____

_____

_____

_____

_____

_____

_____

_____

_____

_____

_____

_____

_____

_____

_____

_____

_____

_____

_____

_____

_____

_____

_____

_____

"Success in marriage does not come merely through finding the right mate, but through being the right mate."

—BARNETT BRICKNER

"I know what love is. It's understanding. It's you and me and let the rest of the world go by."

—DEWITT BODEEN

JOURNAL

_____

_____

_____

_____

_____

_____

_____

_____

_____

_____

_____

_____

_____

_____

_____

_____

"Throw your dreams into space like a kite, and you do not know
what it will bring back, a new life, a new friend, a new love, a
new country."

—ANAÏS NIN

"The best proof of love is trust."

—JOYCE BROTHERS

"Listen to no one who tells you how to love. Your love is like no other, and that is what makes it beautiful."

—PAUL WILLIAMS

> "Love imperfectly. Be a love idiot. . . . Spill things. Tell secrets. . . . Wake up laughing and cry frequently for no reason. Perfection in love is a narrow and suffocating path."
>
> —SARK

> "I love sitting on your lap. I could sit here all day if you didn't stand up."
>
> —GROUCHO MARKS,
> in *Horsefeathers*

_____

_____

_____

_____

_____

_____

_____

_____

_____

_____

_____

_____

_____

_____

_____

_____

"We were together, I have forgotten the rest."

—WALT WHITMAN

Warner Books, Inc., 1271 Avenue of the Americas, New York, NY 10020
Visit our Web site at www.twbookmark.com

 An AOL Time Warner Company

Printed in the United States of America
First Printing: May 2003
10 9 8 7 6 5 4 3 2 1

Library of Congress Cataloging-in-Publication Data

Bridal shower memories.
p.cm.
ISBN 0-446-69060-0
1. Showers (Parties) 2. Bridal books. I. Warner Books (Firm)

GV1472.7.S5 B76 2003
793.2—dc21   2002027443

Concept and text by Sandra Bark

Cover design by Carol Bokuniewicz

Cover and interior illustrations by Shasti O'Leary Soudant

Book design and text composition by Jo Anne Metsch